Professor Murray Henner
Embry-Riddle Aeronautical University- U.S.A.
Mr. Patrick Mernick-Graduate Assistant

A NEW PARADIGM FOR DIAGNOSIS AND TREATMENT OF AIDS IN SOUTH AFRICA UTILIZING A SOCIOLOGICALLY AND GLOBALLY BASED PERSPECTIVE

The pre-parliamentary republic of South Africa terminated in 1994. The issue of addressing repercussions of invidious discrimination becomes problematic in pertinent part because the end of apartheid in 1994 did not address physical and mental health issues that predated the end of colonial rule. However, even with the peaceful transition of power, the AIDS epidemic and failure of social institutions to address the likes of unemployment, hygiene and medical problems is slowly destroying the nation, and may lead to a change in society's structure. Unemployment remains extremely high, as the country has struggled with many changes, some of which are the natural consequences of a society based on isolation and segregation. While many blacks have risen to middle or upper classes, the overall unemployment rate of blacks has significantly increased between 1994 and 2012.

Prior to 1994, descendants of Dutch colonialists, (Afrikaners or Boers), gained political and social control of the country through the Nationalist Party (NP) and fostered a system of apartheid, or separation of the races (Thompson 2000). However, it should be noted that as far back as 1912, the African National Congress (ANC) was established with its' goal to alter society by employing tools for change through civil disobedience and passive resistance. Nelson Mandela became the driving force behind the party, and was imprisoned by the NP in 1960. Due to external economic pressures, and mounting riots and demonstrations, the South African government came to realize the necessity for change. Thereafter, F.W. de Klerk was elected President of South Africa and released Nelson Mandela from incarceration. Together they founded a government that ended apartheid (Tordoff 2002). Though the nation is no longer racially segregated, it still faces the issue of HIV/AIDS, unemployment and a bureaucracy which fails to address social and medical issues to name a few. The AIDS epidemic is ravaging the population, and has had the effect of destroying its' infrastructure.

A similar dilemma may still exist in the United States. For example, Jeff Manza and Christopher Uggen in an article dated September 2004, published by the American Political Association, opine that one of the three key reasons for disenfranchisement is "…the racial dynamics that color both the history and contemporary effects of felon disenfranchisement in the United States." (Manza, et.al. 491). The authors' further suggest that "…Although disenfranchisement laws are facially neutral, historical antecedents and contemporary disparities have created the widespread perception that race underlies the practice." (Manza, et. al 492). Utilizing a rather subjective event-history analysis, the authors subsequently conclude that "…states with larger proportions of nonwhites in their prison population were more likely to pass restrictive laws, even after statistically controlling for the effects of time, region, economic competition between whites and blacks, partisan control of government and punitiveness." (Manza, et. al. 493). Finally, Manza and Uggen conclude in part that there was a significant impact on the African American community (which) suggests both a casual role for race and an important set of race-related impacts as to the origins of felon disenfranchisement laws. (Manza, et. al. 502).

Manza and Uggen have made some substantial leaps of faith in their analysis. For example, Manza and Uggen have not considered that other criminologists have already addressed issues that relate to how segregation (for example), amongst races has already contributed to high rates of victimization. This is still true in South Africa. For example, Min Xie, in her article entitled, "The Effects of Multiple Dimensions of Residential Segregation on Black and Hispanic Homicide Victimization, "published on 23 October 2009 in the Journal of Quantitative Criminology, stated that "…prior to the 1900s, only a few studies explored how segregation may contribute to the high rates of victimization among minorities." (Xie 238). However, it should be noted that the frequently cited Sampson and Graves test of social organization theory based on the British Crime Survey and data conducted in 1982 is now deemed by many criminologists and sociologists as a classic study because it suggests an individual's residence, i.e. the neighborhoods in which a person lives, is more significant than identifiable features such as gender, race and age, in determining the probability an individual will engage in various illegal activities that relate to street crime in a particular geographic location. Thus, although Xie accurately states that "…the analysis's of Hispanic segregation is important for theoretical reasons…Blacks and Hispanics share important structural similarities as they both experience high levels of crime." (Xie 238). This appears to be somewhat problematic in view of Sampson and Graves studies which concluded that gender, race and age is not as significant as an individual's residence in determining causation-victimization levels of deviance. The question thus remains, that the empirical evidence Manza and Uggen have employed appear to overestimate ones race as a cause for disenfranchisement amongst Blacks.

Garland suggests that the foundation and roots of mass imprisonment and its societal repercussions have become an "iron cage and that it is history, demand for public safety, and politicization of the criminal justice system were instrumental in the increment of criminals in our prison systems. If as Garland suggests that the "…criminalized poor may lack political power…they have the negative capacity to make life unpleasant for everyone else." This may be one of the effects of "apartheid." He is quite emotional in his rhetoric that lacks empirical and/or scientific data to suggest that the raison d'etre for mass imprisonment appears to be emphasis on segregation rather than education and other political reform. Similar to Mazza, Uugen and Maurer, Garland appears to stress social control, rather than variables such as race.

It cannot be gainsaid that certain victims must struggle with a myriad of traumas subsequent to the end of apartheid, but must also battle with the ancillary or subordinate injuries. These injuries may occur when there is a lack of proper support. These injuries can be caused by well-wishers who may occupy an inner circle of relatives, friends, and even health care professionals. Furthermore, criminal justice officials such as police, prosecutors, social service agency workers, clergy and psychologists/and psychiatric workers may be instrumental in subliminal victimization. Some of the so-called professionals lack proper training and experience to provide effective assistance to the victim. This may have a setback effect on a victim and even exacerbate the problematic issue of rehabilitation. The now integrated racial mix in South Africa makes it clear that certain victims of apartheid must struggle with a myriad of traumas, both physical and psychological and must also battle with the ancillary or subordinate injuries. These injuries may occur when there is a lack of proper support. These injuries can be caused by well-wishers who may occupy an inner circle of relatives, friends, and even health care professionals. Furthermore, government officials such as police, prosecutors, social service agency workers, clergy and psychologists/and psychiatric workers may be instrumental in subliminal victimization. Some of the so-called professionals lack proper training and experience to provide effective assistance to the victim. This may have a setback effect on a victim and even exacerbate the problematic issue of adapting to a new form of democracy. Frequently these workers lack empathy and do not fully understand the trauma of experiencing not only the event causing a victim to suffer but also how victims become pawns for the state (prosecutors) in bringing an offender to justice

The government in South Africa has made insignificant or woefully inadequate steps to curb the outbreak of a number of diseases, including but not limited to AIDS, and at times has been viewed as an inhibitor to AIDS prevention. In 2000 President Thabo Mbeki spoke to the global community and actually stated "… he did not believe that HIV caused AIDS." A form of denial in part, (perhaps even revisionism) but his stance was also politically motivated. In 1998, the government prophylactically blocked the use of antiretroviral drugs, due to alleged or potential side-effects. Should the government continue to ignore the epidemic, the results could be catastrophic to the nation. "AIDS has been cited as the major cause of premature deaths, with mortality rates increasing by about 79% in the period 1997-2004, with a much higher increase in women than in men. Children are a particularly vulnerable group with high rates of MTCT as well as the impacts of ill health and death of parents, with AIDS contributing about 50% to the problem of orphans in the country. Household level impacts are the most devastating effects of HIV and AIDS in the country. Increases in maternal and childhood mortality are some of the devastating impacts, threatening the country's ability to realize the millennium development goals targets of 2015." (*Department of Health, 2006) See,* BROAD FRAMEWORK FOR HIV & AIDS and STI STRATEGIC PLAN FOR 2007-2011SOUTH AFRICA, NOVEMBER 2006

The Routine Activity Theory can also be applied to a myriad of deviant behaviors still practiced in South Africa. The theory was first developed by Cohen and Felson. It is one of several theories that attempt to explain ways in which specific behaviors are committed. The theory hypothesizes that technology has increased the number of incidents in certain crimes (such as cyber fraud) as an explanation for the increase in exposure to motivated offenders (Pratt. et. al 2010)

The theory has recently been expanded to study and examine more than sociodemographic characteristics and the increased likelihood for fraud online. As technology is a significant part of South Africa's main infrastructure, the authors 'suggest that in the past, criminologists studying sociodemographic variables and their research, offered "… little insight into the casual mechanisms that underlie corruption in the government, fraud targeting and victimization." (Pratt 2010) The theory as designed by Cohen and Felson and their research merely predicted "…aggregate changes in legitimate opportunity structures," (Pratt 2010) but failed to address the theory's impact on routine online activities and the likelihood of internet fraud targeting. Without appearing to be subjective, the theory has particular disadvantages, as past empirical research failed to examine target selection and does not account for the fact that fraud perpetrators target consumers from all backgrounds (Pratt citing Holtfreter et al. 2006). Simply stated, the original theory appears simplistic in its application to a host of criminal activities.

Routine activity theory is based upon the premise that deviant acts originate in the daily routines of everyday life. The theory articulates there must be three elements involved in order for a crime to be committed: a motivated offender, a suitable target and lack of guardianship. (Pratt et. al 2010) It is suggested that certain behaviors can shift from deviant to non-deviant actions. Therefore, who is the motivated offender? Second, who is an intended target? The target can be as diverse as a single offender to that of a large corporate entity or governmental agencies. However, with advanced global internet capabilities, the issue that must be investigated is whether routine online internet activity will increase fraud targeting. The criminal justice system in South Africa has not stepped up to the plate in prosecuting many of the alleged acts of corruption and fraud. These variables may affect intervention and play a role in the prevention of the deviant behavior or the inefficacy of the South African government to deal with epidemics such as AIDS.

According to the routine activity theory, for a crime to occur there must be a convergence in space and time of the three requirements (Akers, 2004) Akers also suggests the premise of the routine activities theory is if there is any lack of one of the three requirements, then a crime will not occur and that he convergence of the requirements is due to the routine activities of people (Akers, 2004).

The theory could also be applied to a study of white-collar crimes, consumers and victimization such as the one Hazel Croall conducted in 2008. The theory has been examined in various crimes. (Croall 2008) However, there remains a poignant question at hand. That query is why the theory fails to account for why some individuals are motivated offenders and some are not. (Akers, 2004). The theory assumes that motivated offenders will just be in a particular place when their target is there and there is a lack of a capable guardian (Akers, 2004).

In Brian Parsi Boetig's article published in the FBI Law Enforcement Bulletin in 2006, he points out that the routine activity theory has been applied to various criminological studies from stalking to narcotic trafficking." (Boetig 2006) Thankfully, Ronald V. Clarke in the attached article has articulated that some criminologist like Zey, in 1998 do not accept the premises of routine activity theory as valid. (Zey, 1998. "…assumptions inherent in rational choice theory are: 1. Humans are purposive and goal oriented; 2. Humans have sets of hierarchically ordered preferences, or utilities; and 3. In choosing lines of behavior, humans make rational calculations with respect to: a. the utility of alternative lines of conduct with reference to the preference hierarchy, b. the costs of each alternative in terms of utilities foregone, and c. the best way to maximize utility.(Clarke citing Jonathan Turner 2008) It is interesting to note that neither Pratt and his co-authors, nor Croall has addressed these concerns.

Today, the rate for AIDS in South Africa, is equal amongst men and women, and there are over 250,000 between the ages of 15 to 35 that die annually. This has left a generation gap, and within twenty years, there will be a deficiency of eligible workers in South Africa, as well as millions of orphans who will have grown up without parents or social education (Landman 2002).

The purpose of this paper is to study the AIDS epidemic in a sociological and criminological context in South Africa; determine if social changes will take place in the future, and explore how sexual attitudes affect group infection rates. This Thesis will explore the problems the nation faces due to apartheid and the AIDS epidemic and inadequacy of the South African social and political bureaucracy, while hypothesizing what might happen to the nation's social institutions

THE SOUTH AFRICAN DELIMA

HIV/AIDS refers to the Human Immunodeficiency Virus and Acquired Immune Deficiency Syndrome respectively. *HIV* destroys the normal functioning of the immune system, which leads to the development of AIDS. This makes a person susceptible to infection and contraction of a myriad of other diseases. *HIV,* has been scientifically established as acquired through the transmission of "infected blood, semen, or vaginal secretions [that] come in contact with an uninfected person's broken skin or mucous membranes" (CDC 2003).

Currently Africa has the largest infection rate of *HNI*AIDS of any continent in the world. Over 70 percent of world AIDS cases are from Africa, and 8,700 Africans are infected with HIV every minute-3.2 million a year. The disease has greatly reduced the average life expectancy to around 40 years of age, and of the 25 million Africans infected, only an estimated 100,000 have access to antiretroviral drugs (World Bank 2002).

It has been argued that the affect that HIV/AIDS is having on Africa has little impact on the rest of the world. In North America, there are only an estimated 1.2 million cases, and in Western Europe, the numbers drop to less than 700,000. While much of the world may view HIV/AIDS as a tragedy little, besides monetary aid relief, is being accomplished to help African nations deal with the epidemic (World Bank 2002). However, it has also been opined that this epidemic obviously affects unemployment, economic policy and ultimately civil unrest.

This leaves few positive outcomes for sovereign states where unstable and corrupt regimes are normal; and while the rest of the continent faces an uncertain future, there is hope in the nation of South Africa. The rather peaceful end of segregation in 1994, and the limited corruption within the government, make it the best candidate for dealing with the epidemic, and gives it a greater chance for a positive outcome, though it will still be a significant challenge. South Africa has seen the number of infected double from 2.4 million in 1997 to over 5 million in 2004 (Hoyle 2004). As stated earlier, both men and women are equally infected, and it is expected that AIDS orphans will reach 2 million, with an expected 7 million AIDS deaths by the end of the decade (Butler 2004).

The nation also faces many of the same problems that the rest of southern Africa faces that contribute to the spread of the virus, such as the influx of migrant labor and prostitution. This produces large concentrations of young men in cities who later return to their families during holidays, or at the end of their contract. While in the cities they take part in the rampant prostitution and contract HIV, spreading it to their wives when they return home (Phillips 2004). In most African cities, the chance of contracting AIDS from a prostitute is 50 percent (Hoyle 2004). The success of prostitution and the spread of infection can be attributed to social norms within the different racial groups of South Africa.

All racial groups within the nation are being impacted by HIV/AIDS: the Blacks, Whites, Coloured, and Indians. Each racial group has dealt with the epidemic within their respective societies; however, the data shows that the Blacks have the highest percentage of prevalence within the nation (Avert.org 2005). This is due to their social practices regarding sex.

The Black population is the majority in South Africa. The term "Black" describes natives of African descent who are further broken up into tribes such as: Zulu, Xhosa, and Khoikhoi. As a whole, however, they share similar customs and ideals, and so will be grouped under one heading (Thompson 2000).

Blacks are the oldest inhabitants of South Africa, and only came into contact with White settlers in the sixteenth century. While each tribe has a diversified history with White settlers, they have all been used as slaves, uprooted from their homelands, and killed off. After the end of Apartheid segregation in 1994, the Blacks – through the ANC- reformed the government and became the political majority for the first time in over 300 years. Today the ANC is still the lead political party in South Africa (Thompson 2000).

Blacks currently have the highest HIV/AIDS infection rates in the nation. They account for over 76 percent of the population, have some of the highest birth rates, and an infection rate of 12.9 percent (Avert 2005). With a nation of over 42 million inhabitants, this means that the Black community makes up 4 million of the 5 million HIV/AIDS cases in South Africa (Butler 2004).

One main reason for the high infection rate is social behavior. AIDS awareness campaigns do not appeal to the Black community, especially because of the cultural acceptance of sexual relations. These campaigns have posted highway signs that read 'Choose life: Practice abstinence.' They try to promote 'behavior change' towards sex, yet have thus far only antagonized the situation. Some women enter into numerous sexual relationships to expel expectations of chastity, or for the gain of consumer items, despite the known risks. Social historians have also noticed that there is a "failure of communication between parents and children on sexual issues" (Carton 2003: 199).

There is also the cultural norm of "wife inheritance." When a woman is widowed, she is taken in by her husband's family for the care of herself, and her children. It is common that inheritors will then enter into sexual relations with this woman. If her husband died of AIDS, then the infected widow will spread the disease to her inheritor, who would then transmit the disease to his wife, who in turn could pass it on to breastfeeding children (Hoyle 2004).

Ignorance of the disease is another contributing factor to the spread of HIV amongst Blacks. One province known as Kwazulu-Natal, where the highest prevalence of the disease is found in South Africa amongst the Zulus, the term AIDS is referred to as the "woman's disease" since women are seen as sexually as promiscuous. A woman who discloses that she is infected faces the threat of being abandoned or killed (Albertyn 2003). This misguided social behavior only fuels the spread of HIV/AIDS amongst the Black community. Whites are the second largest racial group in South Africa. The term "Whites" incorporates the Afrikaners and English. While the two groups differ slightly in their religious and political beliefs, they are still very similar in their social attitude.

In yet another study published by Campbell, (Campbell 1999) Dr. Campbell along with her colleagues, determined the effects of relationships with the legal, medical, and mental health systems and how they affected a victim's psychological and mental health. Their conclusion from this study was also revealing because the results of that study indicated that "…although community services may be beneficial for some victims, there is increasing evidence that they can add trauma, rather than alleviate distress (termed secondary victimization)." (Campbell 1999). The author illustrated the effects of secondary victimization on survivors' posttraumatic stress (PTS) symptoms.

In Campbell's study, samples were used to recruit over one hundred survivors. According to Campbell, et. al, "...victims of non-stranger rape who received minimal assistance from either the legal or medical system, and encountered victim-blaming behaviors from system personnel, had significantly elevated levels of PTS." (Campbell 1999) Such re-victimization is counterproductive because if the mission of specific agencies is to de traumatize and assist victims with rehabilitative therapy, post-traumatic stress levels should not be much greater than other victims in their study, particularly victims who did not seek help from a variety of agencies.

Apparently, the authors' infer that high-risk survivors who receive sustained services had a decrease over time in post-traumatic symptoms. Thus, the question raised is not only what type of services is being offered, but also the length of time the assistance is proffered along with the nature and quality of service. Furthermore, "...although community services may be beneficial for some victims, there is increasing evidence that they can add trauma, rather than alleviate distress (termed secondary victimization)." (Id.) This article illustrated the effects of secondary victimization on survivors' posttraumatic stress (PTS) symptoms. A sample of over one hundred rape victims were engaged in this study. According to Campbell, et. al, "...victims ...who received minimal assistance from either the legal or medical system, and encountered victim-blaming behaviors from system personnel, had significantly elevated levels of PTS." (Id.)

In conclusion, research revealed that if the goal was to assist victims with rehabilitative services, then it would follow that subsequent PST levels would not be greater than other victims in their analysis, particularly victims who did not ask for aid from a variety of social service agencies. Apparently, the authors' infer that high-risk survivors who receive sustained services had a decrease over time in post-traumatic symptoms. Thus, the question raised is not only what type of service is being offered, but also the length of time the assistance is proffered along with the nature and quality of service. PST is still commonplace among citizens of South Africa who experienced apartheid and its repercussions.

The history of the White population begins with the arrival of the Dutch East- Indian Company. South Africa became a colony of the Company in 1652 and acted as a supplying post for ships passing through to Asia. In 1795, the British assumed power and Whites were able to expand further into the region through superior technology, economics, and pitting tribes against each other (Butler 2004). In 1910, South Africa became its own country, and in 1948, the Afrikaners gained control of the government with their Nationalist Party (NP). They were then able to slowly eliminate all Black and colored people's participation in the political system through the policy of Apartheid, or separation of the races (Thompson 2000).

Whites currently have an infection rate far below that of Blacks. They account for about 11 percent of the population, and have a group infection rate of just over 6 percent. This means the White population has 280,000 HIV/AIDS cases. Their lower infection rate can be attributed to their social behavior and attitudes towards sex (Avert 2005).

White social norms prevent them from being sexually promiscuous due to European based religious beliefs that promote abstinence. They have always held the positions of economic and political power in South Africa, which has allowed them to finance proper educations for their children, which have aided them in the teaching of proper moral behavior. They are overwhelmingly Christian with strong Calvinist beliefs within the Dutch Reformed Church.

If the current rate of infection continues amongst Whites, their society will see little change. Even after their change in economic and social standing, Whites have continued to be a powerful force in South Africa. Their infection rates are low, and their religious beliefs do not allow for promiscuity.

The term "Coloured" is used to describe the section of the population that is a mixture of different races. They are mostly found in the Cape area, and after emancipation from slavery in 1834, they began to refer to themselves as the Cape Coloured People. Up until1857, the Coloured were incorporated into Afrikaner society and suffered minimal discrimination. However, pressure from the Dutch Reformed Church forced the beginnings of segregation and a split of the congregation, leading to the establishment of the Uniting Reformed Church for Coloured participation. Coloureds are a very diverse group, both culturally and economically. The formation of the Union of South Africa in 1910 legalized discrimination against Coloureds, which made it difficult for them to compete with Whites for positions (Thompson 2000).

The infection rates amongst the Coloured population are similar to those of the Whites. They constitute 9 percent of the population, and have an infection rate similar to Whites at just over 6 percent. This puts their total population infected at 225,000 (Avert 2005).

The lower rates amongst Coloured compared to Blacks could be associated with their social/cultural similarities to the White population. Despite the prejudice and discrimination they faced after 1910, the long history of being economically and socially similar to Whites became imbedded in their culture. The similarity in culture was also reflected in their similar White sexual attitudes. If the current rate of infection amongst Coloureds continues, their society will see little change (Thompson 2000).

The Indian population is the smallest group in South Africa, and also the newest migrant group. Their population began to flourish in South Africa in the 1860s when the British government began to import them from India to resolve a skilled labor shortage. They are mostly found in on the east coast, especially within the city of Durban where there is a large Indian-based community (Thompson 2000).

The Indian population currently has the lowest infection rates of any group in South Africa. They compose only 3 percent of the population, and have an infection rate of less than 2 percent. This means their infected population stands at only 16,000 people (Avert 2005).

Their low infection rates may be a result of their social behavior with regards to sex. Traditional Hindu beliefs discourage sex before marriage, and it is estimated that 60 percent of men are virgins on their wedding nights. Sex and children are viewed as a stage in life, and the act of adultery can reflect on a person's karma. Although some Indians have changed their religious beliefs (40 percent follow other faiths), imbedded cultural norms are more difficult to alter (Richards 2004). If the Indian infection rate continues to remain below 2 percent, their group will see little impact of the AIDS epidemic.

If South Africa does not deal with the problem of HIV/AIDS, there is the possibility of economic and political instability within the next few decades. A generation gap in the population due to the HIV/AIDS epidemic could result in the prior of these two. Currently the population is undergoing negative population growth due to AIDS. The majority of HIV cases are amongst the reproductive population from the ages of 20-34; which may lead to a generation gap. This generation gap could have a dramatic impact on South Africa within the next few decades, which could lead to lack of skilled employees in the nation, leading to a damaged economy. "As a quarter of skilled workers and perhaps one in seven highly skilled workers become infected by 2005, AIDS will also severely undermine the human capital in the public service, business, and the professions that will be required to address the pandemic's consequences" (Butler 2004: 144). With a lack of opportunities in the job market, a large portion of the professional community has left in search for opportunities in other nations such as Australia, the UK, Canada, and the US. More than 200,000 emigrated in the 1990s, and it is estimated that this number will double by 2010 (Butler 2004). Should this trend continue, the combination of emigrated and dead skilled workers could bring about an economic crisis.

A second generation gap could appear through the loss of children. Those who are breast fed from their infected mothers have a one in third chance of contracting the virus if the mother is not taking azidothymidine (AZT) retroviral drugs (Hoyle 2004). Current access to AZT drugs is limited in South Africa with only 1.4 million people currently receiving treatment. Often, it is unknown whether or not a child has been infected by his dead mother, and the child is abandoned (Sidley 2003).

Economic instability within African nations tends to lead to corruption, as can be seen in neighboring Zimbabwe. Its drastic economic decline over the last two decades has turned the nation into an autocratic regime. Though this is a faint possibility for South Africa, there will undoubtedly be a change within its society due to the AIDS epidemic.

The religious community has tried to help bring about AIDS awareness through reaching out to the community. They have a history of community service, and has served in South Africa as a mediator between colonizers and Blacks. When Coloured children were banned from public school is 1857, mission institutions opened their doors to educating them (Thompson 2000).

The two largest religious organizations are the Zion Christian Church, with over 4 million members, and the Dutch Reformed Churches, with a combined membership of almost 4 million. The latter was considered to be the national religion during apartheid and followed the NP political agenda. Many religious organizations, such as the

Methodist Church, Catholic Church, and Anglican Church aided in the end of apartheid, although many members left the Catholic and Anglican Churches in support of apartheid policies (Butler 2004).

Today these religious organizations try to educate the population on the hazards of HIV/AIDS. This can be seen through the growing Zion Christian Church that accepts the traditional beliefs of the Africans, and as a result has built a large following since 1990. They condemn the consumption of alcoholic beverages, smoking, sexual promiscuity, and violence (Butler 2004). The Catholic Church also condemns sexual promiscuity, and is against the government handing out condoms. The Anglican Church has taken this stance on condoms as well, and in January 2005, they announced the beginning of "Teaching Our Children" program which is aimed at teaching abstinence amongst the younger generations (iafrica 2005b)

No matter what the current program against AIDS in South Africa is, the current rate of infection will lead to a shift in the nation's society. This could lead to a shift in the nation's political structure since history shows-through the example of apartheid- that social turmoil leads to political change.

Apartheid began in 1948 when Afrikaner nationalists came to power. The program encouraged "separate development of the races" which lead to the placement of Blacks into homelands (Tordoff 2002, 65).

In places where the African nationalist movement was able to flourish, the African social upheaval against townships and segregation policies led to the eventual fall of apartheid and a change in the government's structure (Tordoff 2002). The government today is still headed by the ANC; however, their attempts to control the epidemic have not been successful. They are viewed both domestically and internationally as being inept. The following will examine the government's successes and failures.

The transition of power in 1994 delayed the response time to the outbreak of the virus, and has resulted in some questionable policymaking with regards to HIV/AIDS. During the first few years of the new government, President Mandela desegregated the prisons' infected from uninfected, and began the distribution of condoms to all prisoners. The policy of prison segregation, under the apartheid regime, controlled the outbreak of AIDS within the prisons; however, since the ANC was desegregating the rest of society, it only goes to follow that this course of action would extend to all aspects of government services. The ANC had a different stance on AIDS compared to the Afrikaners, and even "overturned the policy of the police, correctional services and defense force to carry out HIV testing on all new applicants for jobs" (Phillips 2004: 42). Whites were concerned about the disease, and even went so far as to test their Black workers for fear they might infect family members. Meanwhile, young Black activists considered the virus another propaganda ploy by the government in the last days of apartheid to stop the African nationalist movement. Some even called AIDS the acronym for "Afrikaner Invention to Deprive us of Sex," and Blacks paid little heed to the disease (Phillips 2004: 34).

Since the end of capital punishment, the integration of infected prisoners is a dangerous choice. Many incarcerated individuals have not even gone to trial yet to decide their fate. Approximately 23 percent of those being held are still in the pre-trial phase. If set free, these innocent people have possibly contracted the AIDS virus, and could reenter society and infect more of the population (Human 2004). Crime in general has risen since the transition of power, and South Africa is one of the largest rape capitals of the world. From September 2002 to August 2003, almost 23 percent of South Africans reported being a victim of crime.

Secondary victimization has been defined by one criminologist, R. Campbell, in her article entitled, "Secondary victimization of rape victims: insights from mental health professionals who treat survivors of violence." Secondary victimization has been determined to be a repercussion of repeated instances of is frequently the result of the shock of sexual incursions of abuse or rape victims. The article illustrates that such repeated disturbances is a secondary repercussion of several types of assaults which happens through the responses of individuals and institutions to the victim. There are many types of secondary victimization. These include but are not limited to victim blaming, inappropriate behavior or language by medical personnel and by other organizations with access to the victim post assault. (See, Campbell 1989) Several studies have indicated that many survivors may be receiving benign forms of assistance from the criminal justice system but these same survivors become ill-treated by the same agencies whose mission is to help victims. In one particular study conducted by Dr. Campbell, a probability sampling was used to survey a representative sample of licensed mental health professionals about the extent to which they believe rape victims are subjected to destructive and/or violent and abusive behavior in their interactions with social system personnel. Campbell's findings are startling. Research revealed that many health care professionals actually engage in harmful behavior detrimental to the "victim." (Campbell, 1999)

It is estimated that more than half of the crime that takes place is actually reported (Burton 2004). In 2000, there were over 50,000 rape cases reported, and if this accounts for only half, then it can be assumed that over 100,000 cases of rape actually took place (Amnesty 2003). This would also put South Africa's crime rate from September 2002 to August 2003 at over 46 percent (Burton 2004).

While these changes to policy and society may be seen as destructive to South Africa, the ANC has tried multiple tactics to educate the people of South Africa to prevent such damage. Upon entering the office of Presidency, Mandela doubled the government budget for AIDS Awareness programs, extended them to public schools, began condom distribution, and increased media attention. The ANC also stopped the testing of HIV/AIDS amongst incoming hospital patients, since it was seen as an infringement to human rights which could prevent someone from obtaining proper medical care (Phillips 2004: 42).

However, the cycle has begun again, and President Mbeki is now facing the same criticisms Mandela did. Mbeki is seen as not supporting intellectual property rights in his attempt to bring in AZT drugs to South Africa. In 2001, 39 pharmaceutical companies took the government to court over legislation that would give the government the power to manufacture generics of brand-name drugs. The cost in 2001 for the combination of drugs needed to treat the disease was over $1,000 a month per patient (BBC 2001). Other options are available to the government besides the procurement of expensive AZT drugs, such as basic vitamin supplements, which some studies have shown can also reduce the chance of transmission, although even these have become hard to come by (Bering 2000). The drug companies eventually dropped their case, and under the Trade Related Aspects of Intellectual Property Rights, the government can produce and sell products with patents without the compliance of the patent holder (Barrow 2001). While this allows cheap drugs to be distributed and possibly curtail the spread of infection, it also prevents companies from investing in South Africa-especially those with patents they would like to protect.

In 2000, President Thabo Mbeki stated to the world that he did not consider AIDS to be the largest health threat facing South Africa, and doubted HIV even caused AIDS. He cited poorer socio-economic classes as being the contributing factor since they have higher infection rate. This statement lead to African AIDS activists and the Congress of South African Trade Unions to threaten a civil disobedience campaign should the government not discuss the provision of AZT drugs (Hunter 2003). It is true that those from lower incomes tend to have more risky sexual experiences, diminished access to health information which can lead to a delayed diagnosis and treatment, and lowered concern about one's future health; however, it is more likely Mbeki was playing a political game (Fassin 2003). The government views AIDS differently than it views other diseases, such as malaria. The South African government sees malaria as curable, and therefore worth the cost of prevention, generally through the use of DDT sprays. In contrast, HIV/AIDS is a disease that can be hidden from the infected individual, and most importantly, is not curable (Bering 2000).

Even if the government did show full support towards aiding HIV/AIDS patients, it could never afford to provide its entire infected population with AZT drugs. If South Africa were to purchase AZT retroviral drugs, it would use up the entire public health budget of the nation – and that only accounts for those patients that have admitted to being infected with HIV/AIDS. While the number stands at 5 million, in reality, the numbers could be much higher (Bering 2000).

Current supplies of antiviral drugs are being poorly distributed in South Africa. There have even been cases of child rape victims not having access to AZT drugs because they are not available. It is especially difficult for children (who account for 40 percent of rape victims) to obtain the drugs since parental permission is needed (BBC 2004). However, distribution today is far better than in the 1990s when the ANC government blocked the use of antiretroviral drugs due to their concern for possible side-effects, and refused to give pregnant women drugs even though AZT was proven "to be effective at staving off the fatal complications of the virus" (Moeller 2000: 89). More than half of HIV positive women choose to carry their pregnancy to term (Plessis 2003). This treatment has been proven to greatly reduce the transmission of HIV from mother to child through pregnancy and breastfeeding, which accounts for 10% of the annual infection rates (Makgoba 2000).

Children that do not acquire the virus from their mothers, whom die, end up becoming orphans. The government has acknowledged the need to care and provide for AIDS orphans, but currently the programs in place are limited, and are only a temporary solution with no long-term goals.

This continued growth of orphans is a dangerous situation. The current social response to this is family adoption. Blacks have a tradition known as Ubuntu where the relatives or even neighbors will see to the child's basic needs. However, there is a stigma attached to children orphaned by AIDS, and they are often times ostracized by society, even if they are not infected. Those who are not taken in by family are often forced to fend for themselves. Young girls begin prostituting, and boys join gangs and add to South Africa's colossal crime rates. The government currently has a Foster Care Grant in place which distributes R410 ($66 USD) monthly to foster parents willing to take in orphans to AIDS parents. Unfortunately, the system can take up to two years to distribute money to families in need (Landman 2002).

The most difficult issue the government faces in order to control the spread of AIDS is the changing of social norms regarding sex. Perhaps, the Black's view on sex which has lead to their highest infection rate compared to other groups. Indians, who have a very strict cultural view on sex, have the least amount of infection. A solution is needed that will set up domestic programs which will focus on behavior modification towards sexual attitudes.

The solution to the AIDS epidemic in South Africa currently being implemented by the government is one of plausible denial. Thabo Mbeki's 2000 speech, addressed to the world, stated that he did not believe that HIV caused AIDS. In 1998, the ANC government blocked the use of antiretroviral drugs, due to their concern for possible side- effects. If the government argues the facts behind AIDS and its treatments, then it has no need support possible treatments; for example, they would not have to provide AZT drugs if they deny that HIV causes AIDS.

Their current solution allows the government to put off its responsibility to the people, has damaged its image abroad, and has prevented outside donors who are reluctant to back HIVIAIDS

programs when the leadership of South Africa is seen as questioning known treatments. Recently, the

government changed its tune and began the distribution of AZT drugs to 1.4 million of the 5 million

infected. However, this does little to stop the growth of the epidemic, and it is estimated that another

400,000 people will become infected before the program finishes its first year (Sidley 2003).

This solution will not solve the HIV/AIDS crisis in South Africa, and has the nation heading

towards disaster. With the expectation that AIDS orphans will reach 2 million, and the AIDS death toll

will reach 7 million by 2010, there will be considerable social and economic turmoil (Butler 2004).

The best solution for South Africa's future is to come to an understanding that nothing can be

done to help those infected, but the future can still be stabilized through tough government action that

calls for a change to current AIDS awareness programs and an attempt to teach behavior modification

rather than simply passing out condoms and condoning promiscuous sexual relationships. The

promotion of abstinence should be the government's key campaign against HIVIAIDS. This solution

will affect the nations: economics, crime, drug provisions, social behavior and sexual attitudes, and

provide an answer for dealing with the inevitable 2 million orphans. This solution will also focus the

government on long-term containment of HIV/AIDS, while trying to prevent the nation from going

bankrupt.

The problem with this solution is that it is not the most humanitarian method. Since the

government will fundamentally be ignoring the impending deaths of 5 million of its citizens it is likely

the international community - mostly the western world - will see this solution as barbaric. At the

same time though, perhaps the South African government will finally gain some respect for being

rational about the disease.

There is also the chance that this solution will fail, in which case the nation will be left with

millions of orphans without social guidance and further add to domestic problems. The economy could

never recover from the deaths of skilled labor, and could fall into further disarray. Crime, which has become a normal occurrence within the nation, could continue to run rampant, even after the changes have been implemented. Lastly, there is the chance that sexual behavior changes could fail and the Black community could continue with lax sexual attitudes, thus continuing the transmission cycle.

However, with this solution, once the government realizes it cannot save the 5 million infected, they will be able to focus their resources on providing for the future stability of South Africa. The first step is to begin improvements to the nation's economic structure. "While citizens have remained sympathetic towards the government's difficulties in extending public services, the lack of employment opportunities has been a matter of profound and growing dissatisfaction for South Africans of all classes" (Butler 2004: 62). After the change in government in 1994, the nation has seen slow economic growth accompanied by steady population growth (Butler 2004). Incentives to new industry and foreign investors could bring the much-needed business into South Africa.

The government should rethink its stance on its intellectual property rights laws in order to bring in foreign investors. Unfortunately, the current crime rate is keeping many skilled laborers out of South Africa, and until something is done about this, it is unlikely the emigrated and skilled South Africans will return. Crime and economics are mixed and, theoretically, once job opportunities become available to the masses, crime will begin to fall.

Next, the solution would call for a re-education of the population on sexual attitudes and behaviors, and how AIDS awareness is taught. The current sexual norms within the Black community will only further impede the challenge against HN/AIDS. However, as seen in Uganda, these norms can be changed. The country was able to reduce its infection rate from 29 percent to fewer than 5 percent within a decade. Their government did not distribute condoms, as South Africa does; instead, they focused on campaigning abstinence (iafrica 2005a). The distribution of condoms only negates any attempt at promoting abstinence, and gives the appearance that condoms are the foolproof method of preventing transmission, when in fact it is still under debate at just how effective they are. By changing the populations attitude through new awareness campaigns there would be a lower infection rate, which would help curtail the cycle of transmission.

Stopping transmission would be further aided by the government giving AZT drug priority to breastfeeding mothers. They should be given priority access to drugs, in order to prevent the spread of disease to their children. These orphaned children should be given the attention they need to prevent them from enter into lives of crime and prostitution. Current programs for foster children in place are limited, funding of only $66 a month, and delay in money distribution needs to be expanded upon to deal with the coming 2 million orphans. The program should provide more money and resources, in a timely manner, to those providing foster care. More orphanages should be established, both private and state-run, to raise and educate AIDS orphans. Establishing these organizations would allow the government or community organizations to give each child a chance at an education and modify cultural behavior.

Sexual behavior modification could be further aided by setting up programs to rid stigmas attached to HIVIAIDS victims and their children. Mandela has taken a lead role in the awareness of AIDS in South Africa. The recent death of his son due to AIDS, and his outreach into the AIDS community, has been instrumental in awareness. Slowly he and others are changing the stigmas associated with AIDS.

This solution, should it succeed, will provide the government with a stable future consisting of changed social norms regarding sex, and a generation of children raised by the state. It will allow the government to accept that those infected cannot be cured, but future generations can benefit from proper HIV/AIDS awareness.

The HIV/AIDS epidemic is slowly destroying the nation of South Africa. With over 5 million currently infected, and the numbers rising each year, the government has made little attempt to curb the outbreak, and at times has been seen as an inhibitor. With the lack of resources to deal with the disease and its consequences, and the high infection rates amongst the Black community, there will be a major upheaval in the structure of South African society as an entire generation is allowed to die, and millions more are allowed to become infected.

South Africa currently has over 5 million people infected with HIV/AIDS and over 4 million of those are from the sizable Black community. Other racial groups within the society, such as the Whites, Coloureds, and Indians, have a much lower percentage of infected within their communities. This is due to social attitudes regarding sexuality. Blacks are more sexually open and promiscuous, and therefore have higher rates. The other groups have imbedded attitudes that support abstinence.

The South African government has tried futilely to contain the epidemic through sexual programs that are aimed at teaching "safe sex" through condom use. They have also implemented policies that seem to only aid the virus in spreading, such as integration of HIV positive prisoners with non-infected prisoners. The new policy that gives the government access to product patents, for the production of cheap AZT drugs, has kept international investment into South Africa low, as has the high national crime rates. Current production of AZT drugs is very low, and does not give priority to breastfeeding mothers. They have a one-in-three chance of infecting their breastfeeding children.

The most feasible solution for the government of South Africa is to understand that nothing can be done to help those currently infected, and switch awareness programs to promote behavioral changes in sexual attitudes, rather than condoning promiscuity. The government should also focus its attention to the 2 million AIDS orphans that are expected before 2010. These children could easily turn to lives of crime or prostitution, but with the correct foster care in place, they could have productive futures within South African society. The ability for the government to access national patents should be revoked to allow for further international investment and, hopefully, an increase in the economy. With this increase in economy, crime rates should theoretically fall.

This solution, however, could fail. It could give the government a negative image internationally since it will fundamentally be ignoring the impending deaths of 5 million of its citizens. There is also the chance that the orphan programs will fail, in which case the nation will be left with millions of children without social guidance and further add to domestic problems. There is the possibility that the economy would not turn for the better, and crime rates could continue to grow. Finally, there is the chance that behavior modification will not take hold within the Black community, and the epidemic will continue to grow.

Even with this said, this last solution is the nation's best hope. It has been tested and proven in Uganda were the country was able to reduce its infection rate from 29 percent to fewer than 5 percent within a decade. Their government did not distribute condoms, as South Africa does; instead, they focused on campaigning abstinence. They faced all the same troubles South Africa currently does, and were able to overcome the epidemic.

This paper was not intended to fully penetrate the sexual and social attitudes of each group. Other explanations could be given for lower infection rates within some groups, especially that of the Coloureds who are in limbo between White and Blacks. An extensive study could be performed on each of these groups further. However, this Thesis does explain, in detail, Black social norms and gives good examples of traditions that have facilitated the infection rate amongst the group.

The following are problematic issues that have been marshaled during the process of this paper:

- What does recent research say about Blacks being more easily infected with HIV/AIDS than Whites?
- What would be the estimated population of each racial group with current growing infection rates and infant mortality for 2025?
- How is White emigration affecting future prospects of the nation?
- What types of companies have expressed their concern over South Africa's patent laws, and have they declined entering into business in the nation due to them?

WORKS CITED

Albertyn, C. (2003). Contesting democracy: *HNI*AIDS and the achievement of gender equality

    in South Africa. [electronic version] *Feminist Studies, 29(3),* 595-616

Amnesty. (2003). Amnesty International. Amnesty International Report: South Africa. [electronic

    version] Retrieved on April17, 2005 from http://web.amnesty.org/web/web.nsf/report2003/zaf-

    summary- eng/$FILE/south%20africa.pdf

ANC. (2004, 24 March). African National Congress. Maps Index. Retrieved on April18, 2005 from

    http://www.anc.org.zallists/maplist.html

Avert. (2005, 21 March). South Africa HIVIAIDS statistics. Retrieved on March 26, 2005 from

    http://www.avert.org/safricastats.htm

Barrow, G. (2001, 19 April). BBC News. *Cheaper drugs a long way off.* Retrieved on March 28, 2005

    from http://news.bbc.co.uk/1/hi/world/africa/1285616.stm

BBC. (2001, 19 April). BBC News. *SA victory in AIDS drugs case.* Retrieved on March 28, 2005 from

    http://news.bbc.co.uk/1/hilworld/africa/1285097.stm

BBC. (2004, 4 March). BBC News. *SA 'failing rape victims on AIDS.* Retrieved on March 28, 2005

    from http://news.bbc.co.uk/1/hi/world/africa/3532071.stm

Bering, H. (2000, May). *AIDS in South Africa.* The Washington Times, pp. 15

Burton, P.; duPlessis, A.; Leggettt,T.; Louw,A.; Mistry,D.; and van Vuuren, H. (2004, July). Institute

    for Security Studies. Crime levels in South Africa. [electronic version] Retrieved on March 28,

    2005 from http://www.iss.co.zalpubs/Monographs/No101/Chap6.htm

Butler, A. (2004). Contemporary South Africa. New York: Palgrave Macmillian. Carton, B. (2003).

    The forgotten compass of death: Apocalypse then and now in the social history of South

    Africa. The Journal of Social History, 37 (1), 1999

Campbell R, Raja S. (1999) Secondary victimization of rape victims: insights from mental health

    professionals who treat survivors of violence. Violence Vict. 14(3):261-75.

CDC. (2005, 17 February). Center for Disease Control. Frequently asked questions on HIVIAIDS.

Retrieved on March 28, 2005 from http://www.cdc.gov/hiv/pubs/faqs.htm#definition

Fassin, D. & Schneider, H. (2003, 1 March). The politics of AIDS in South Africa: Beyond the controversies. British Medical Journal (International edition), 326 (7387), 495-498.

Hattendorf, J., & Tollerud, T.R. (1997). Domestic Violence: Counseling Strategies That Minimize the Impact of Secondary Victimization. Journal Perspectives in Psychiatric Care, 33(1), 14-23

Hoyle, B. (2004). AIDSIHIV. Farmington Hills, MI: The Gale Group.

Human Rights Watch. (1994, 1 February). Prison Conditions in South Africa. [electronic version] Human Rights Watch.

Hunter, S. (2003). Black Death: AIDS in Africa. New York, NY: Palgrave Macmillian. iafrica. (2005, 24 January). iafrica.com. Condom strategy 'clearly not working'. Retrieved on March 28, 2005. http://africa.iafrica.com/pls/procs/SEARCH.ARCHIVE?p_content_id=367495&p site id=2

iafrica. (2005b, 12 January). iafrica.com. Church to launch $10m HIV/Aids plan. Retrieved on March 28, 2005 from

http://africa.iafrica.com/pls/procs/SEARCH.ARCHIVE?p_content_id=159792&p site id=2

Landman, C. (2002, Nov). The AIDS Orphans of South Africa. Contemporary Review, 281 (1642), 268.

Makogba, M. (2000, 19 May). HIV/AIDS: The peril of pseudoscience. Science, 288 (5469), 1171.

McCubbins, M. D. and Thies, M. F. (1996). Rationality and the Foundations of Positive Political Theory. [Online] Available: http://polisciexplab.ucsd.edu/mccubbin/current/ratcho.htm

Moeller, S. (Fall2000). Coverage of AIDS in Africa: The media are silent no longer. Nieman Reports, 54 (3), 89.

Phillips, H. (2004). HIV/AIDS in the context of South Africa's epidemic history. In Kauffman, K. & Lindauer, D. (Ed.) (2004). AIDS and South Africa: The social expression of a pandemic. Wellesley, MA: Palgrave Macmillian.

Plessis, G. (2003). HIV and fertility in South Africa: Some theoretical and methodological considerations. Department of Social Development. (2003). Fertility: Current South African

    issues of poverty, HIV/AIDS & youth. Cape Town, South Africa: HSRC Publishers.

Richards, S. (2004). Faithnet. Hindu attitudes to sex. Retrieved on March 28, 2005 from

    http://www.faithnet.org.uk/KS4/Marriage%20and%20the%20Familylhindusex.ht m

Sidley, P. (2003). South Africa introduces the world's largest AIDS treatment plan. British Medical

    Journal, 327 (7426), 1246.

Thompson, L. (2000). A History of South Africa. (3rd ed.). USA: Yale University Press.

Tordoff, W. (2002). Government and politics in Africa. (4th ed.). Bloomington, IN: Indiana University

    Press.

TravelSource (n.d). Retrieved March 28, 2005 from

    http://www.travelsource.nl/story/africa/zawolt/zuidafrika.asp?travelreportid=46&

    destinationid=501

World Bank. (2002). World Bank Group. Intensifying action against HIVIAIDS in Africa.

    Retrieved on April 2, 2005 from http://www.worldbank.org/afr/aids/overview.htm

APPENDIX

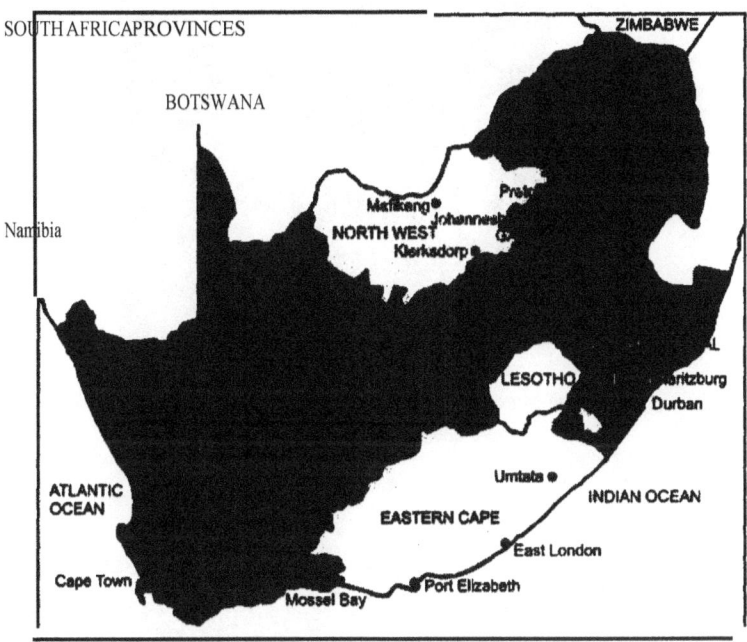

Figure 2: Provinces of South Africa. (Source: ANC, 2004)

Figure 3: Thabo Mbeki, Nelson Mandela, and F.W. de Klerk. (Source: South Africa Travel, 2005).

Figure 4: The South African Flag.(Travel Source, n.d.).

Professor Murray Henner
Embry-Riddle Aeronautical University- U.S.A.
Mr. Patrick Mernick-Graduate Assistant

A NEW PARADIGM FOR DIAGNOSIS AND TREATMENT OF AIDS IN SOUTH

AFRICA UTILIZING A SOCIOLOGICALLY AND GLOBALLY BASED

PERSPECTIVE

The pre-parliamentary republic of South Africa terminated in 1994. The issue of addressing repercussions of invidious discrimination becomes problematic in pertinent part because the end of apartheid in 1994 did not address physical and mental health issues that predated the end of colonial rule. However, even with the peaceful transition of power, the AIDS epidemic and failure of social institutions to address the likes of unemployment, hygiene and medical problems is slowly destroying the nation, and may lead to a change in society's structure. Unemployment remains extremely high, as the country has struggled with many changes, some of which are the natural consequences of a society based on isolation and segregation. While many blacks have risen to middle or upper classes, the overall unemployment rate of blacks has significantly increased between 1994 and 2012.

Prior to 1994, descendants of Dutch colonialists, (Afrikaners or Boers), gained political and social control of the country through the Nationalist Party (NP) and fostered a system of apartheid, or separation of the races (Thompson 2000). However, it should be noted that as far back as 1912, the African National Congress (ANC) was established with its' goal to alter society by employing tools for change through civil disobedience and passive resistance. Nelson Mandela became the driving force behind the party, and was imprisoned by the NP in 1960. Due to external economic pressures, and mounting riots and demonstrations, the South African government came to realize the necessity for change. Thereafter, F.W. de Klerk was elected President of South Africa and released Nelson Mandela from incarceration. Together they founded a government that ended apartheid (Tordoff 2002). Though the nation is no longer racially segregated, it still faces the issue of HIV/AIDS, unemployment and a bureaucracy which fails to address social and medical issues to name a few. The AIDS epidemic is ravaging the population, and has had the effect of destroying its' infrastructure.

A similar dilemma may still exist in the United States. For example, Jeff Manza and Christopher Uggen in an article dated September 2004, published by the American Political Association, opine that one of the three key reasons for disenfranchisement is "…the racial dynamics that color both the history and contemporary effects of felon disenfranchisement in the United States." (Manza, et.al. 491). The authors' further suggest that "…Although disenfranchisement laws are facially neutral, historical antecedents and contemporary disparities have created the widespread perception that race underlies the practice." (Manza, et. al 492). Utilizing a rather subjective event-history analysis, the authors subsequently conclude that "…states with larger proportions of nonwhites in their prison population were more likely to pass restrictive laws, even after statistically controlling for the effects of time, region, economic competition between whites and blacks, partisan control of government and punitiveness." (Manza, et. al. 493). Finally, Manza and Uggen conclude in part that there was a significant impact on the African American community (which) suggests both a casual role for race and an important set of race-related impacts as to the origins of felon disenfranchisement laws. (Manza, et. al. 502).

Manza and Uggen have made some substantial leaps of faith in their analysis. For example, Manza and Uggen have not considered that other criminologists have already addressed issues that relate to how segregation (for example), amongst races has already contributed to high rates of victimization. This is still true in South Africa. For example, Min Xie, in her article entitled, "The Effects of Multiple Dimensions of Residential Segregation on Black and Hispanic Homicide Victimization, "published on 23 October 2009 in the Journal of Quantitative Criminology, stated that "…prior to the 1900s, only a few studies explored how segregation may contribute to the high rates of victimization among minorities." (Xie 238). However, it should be noted that the frequently cited Sampson and Graves test of social organization theory based on the British Crime Survey and data conducted in 1982 is now deemed by many criminologists and sociologists as a classic study because it suggests an individual's residence, i.e. the neighborhoods in which a person lives, is more significant than identifiable features such as gender, race and age, in determining the probability an individual will engage in various illegal activities that relate to street crime in a particular geographic location. Thus, although Xie accurately states that "…the analysis's of Hispanic segregation is important for theoretical reasons…Blacks and Hispanics share important structural similarities as they both experience high levels of crime." (Xie 238). This appears to be somewhat problematic in view of Sampson and Graves studies which concluded that gender, race and age is not as significant as an individual's residence in determining causation-victimization levels of deviance. The question thus remains, that the empirical evidence Manza and Uggen have employed appear to overestimate ones race as a cause for disenfranchisement amongst Blacks.

Garland suggests that the foundation and roots of mass imprisonment and its societal repercussions have become an "iron cage and that it is history, demand for public safety, and politicization of the criminal justice system were instrumental in the increment of criminals in our prison systems. If as Garland suggests that the "…criminalized poor may lack political power…they have the negative capacity to make life unpleasant for everyone else." This may be one of the effects of "apartheid." He is quite emotional in his rhetoric that lacks empirical and/or scientific data to suggest that the raison d'etre for mass imprisonment appears to be emphasis on segregation rather than education and other political reform. Similar to Mazza, Uugen and Maurer, Garland appears to stress social control, rather than variables such as race.

It cannot be gainsaid that certain victims must struggle with a myriad of traumas subsequent to the end of apartheid, but must also battle with the ancillary or subordinate injuries. These injuries may occur when there is a lack of proper support. These injuries can be caused by well-wishers who may occupy an inner circle of relatives, friends, and even health care professionals. Furthermore, criminal justice officials such as police, prosecutors, social service agency workers, clergy and psychologists/and psychiatric workers may be instrumental in subliminal victimization. Some of the so-called professionals lack proper training and experience to provide effective assistance to the victim. This may have a setback effect on a victim and even exacerbate the problematic issue of rehabilitation. The now integrated racial mix in South Africa makes it clear that certain victims of apartheid must struggle with a myriad of traumas, both physical and psychological and must also battle with the ancillary or subordinate injuries. These injuries may occur when there is a lack of proper support. These injuries can be caused by well-wishers who may occupy an inner circle of relatives, friends, and even health care professionals. Furthermore, government officials such as police, prosecutors, social service agency workers, clergy and psychologists/and psychiatric workers may be instrumental in subliminal victimization. Some of the so-called professionals lack proper training and experience to provide effective assistance to the victim. This may have a setback effect on a victim and even exacerbate the problematic issue of adapting to a new form of democracy. Frequently these workers lack empathy and do not fully understand the trauma of experiencing not only the event causing a victim to suffer but also how victims become pawns for the state (prosecutors) in bringing an offender to justice

The government in South Africa has made insignificant or woefully inadequate steps to curb the outbreak of a number of diseases, including but not limited to AIDS, and at times has been viewed as an inhibitor to AIDS prevention. In 2000 President Thabo Mbeki spoke to the global community and actually stated "... he did not believe that HIV caused AIDS." A form of denial in part, (perhaps even revisionism) but his stance was also politically motivated. In 1998, the government prophylactically blocked the use of antiretroviral drugs, due to alleged or potential side-effects. Should the government continue to ignore the epidemic, the results could be catastrophic to the nation. "AIDS has been cited as the major cause of premature deaths, with mortality rates increasing by about 79% in the period 1997-2004, with a much higher increase in women than in men. Children are a particularly vulnerable group with high rates of MTCT as well as the impacts of ill health and death of parents, with AIDS contributing about 50% to the problem of orphans in the country. Household level impacts are the most devastating effects of HIV and AIDS in the country. Increases in maternal and childhood mortality are some of the devastating impacts, threatening the country's ability to realize the millennium development goals targets of 2015." (*Department of Health, 2006) See,* BROAD FRAMEWORK FOR HIV & AIDS and STI STRATEGIC PLAN FOR 2007-2011SOUTH AFRICA, NOVEMBER 2006

The Routine Activity Theory can also be applied to a myriad of deviant behaviors still practiced in South Africa. The theory was first developed by Cohen and Felson. It is one of several theories that attempt to explain ways in which specific behaviors are committed. The theory hypothesizes that technology has increased the number of incidents in certain crimes (such as cyber fraud) as an explanation for the increase in exposure to motivated offenders (Pratt. et. al 2010)

The theory has recently been expanded to study and examine more than sociodemographic characteristics and the increased likelihood for fraud online. As technology is a significant part of South Africa's main infrastructure, the authors 'suggest that in the past, criminologists studying sociodemographic variables and their research, offered "… little insight into the casual mechanisms that underlie corruption in the government, fraud targeting and victimization." (Pratt 2010) The theory as designed by Cohen and Felson and their research merely predicted "…aggregate changes in legitimate opportunity structures," (Pratt 2010) but failed to address the theory's impact on routine online activities and the likelihood of internet fraud targeting. Without appearing to be subjective, the theory has particular disadvantages, as past empirical research failed to examine target selection and does not account for the fact that fraud perpetrators target consumers from all backgrounds (Pratt citing Holtfreter et al. 2006). Simply stated, the original theory appears simplistic in its application to a host of criminal activities.

Routine activity theory is based upon the premise that deviant acts originate in the daily routines of everyday life. The theory articulates there must be three elements involved in order for a crime to be committed: a motivated offender, a suitable target and lack of guardianship. (Pratt et. al 2010) It is suggested that certain behaviors can shift from deviant to non-deviant actions. Therefore, who is the motivated offender? Second, who is an intended target? The target can be as diverse as a single offender to that of a large corporate entity or governmental agencies. However, with advanced global internet capabilities, the issue that must be investigated is whether routine online internet activity will increase fraud targeting. The criminal justice system in South Africa has not stepped up to the plate in prosecuting many of the alleged acts of corruption and fraud. These variables may affect intervention and play a role in the prevention of the deviant behavior or the inefficacy of the South African government to deal with epidemics such as AIDS.

According to the routine activity theory, for a crime to occur there must be a convergence in space and time of the three requirements (Akers, 2004) Akers also suggests the premise of the routine activities theory is if there is any lack of one of the three requirements, then a crime will not occur and that he convergence of the requirements is due to the routine activities of people (Akers, 2004).

The theory could also be applied to a study of white-collar crimes, consumers and victimization such as the one Hazel Croall conducted in 2008. The theory has been examined in various crimes. (Croall 2008) However, there remains a poignant question at hand. That query is why the theory fails to account for why some individuals are motivated offenders and some are not. (Akers, 2004). The theory assumes that motivated offenders will just be in a particular place when their target is there and there is a lack of a capable guardian (Akers, 2004).

In Brian Parsi Boetig's article published in the FBI Law Enforcement Bulletin in 2006, he points out that the routine activity theory has been applied to various criminological studies from stalking to narcotic trafficking." (Boetig 2006) Thankfully, Ronald V. Clarke in the attached article has articulated that some criminologist like Zey, in 1998 do not accept the premises of routine activity theory as valid. (Zey, 1998. "...assumptions inherent in rational choice theory are: 1. Humans are purposive and goal oriented; 2. Humans have sets of hierarchically ordered preferences, or utilities; and 3. In choosing lines of behavior, humans make rational calculations with respect to: a. the utility of alternative lines of conduct with reference to the preference hierarchy, b. the costs of each alternative in terms of utilities foregone, and c. the best way to maximize utility.(Clarke citing Jonathan Turner 2008) It is interesting to note that neither Pratt and his co-authors, nor Croall has addressed these concerns.

Today, the rate for AIDS in South Africa, is equal amongst men and women, and there are over 250,000 between the ages of 15 to 35 that die annually. This has left a generation gap, and within twenty years, there will be a deficiency of eligible workers in South Africa, as well as millions of orphans who will have grown up without parents or social education (Landman 2002).

The purpose of this paper is to study the AIDS epidemic in a sociological and criminological context in South Africa; determine if social changes will take place in the future, and explore how sexual attitudes affect group infection rates. This Thesis will explore the problems the nation faces due to apartheid and the AIDS epidemic and inadequacy of the South African social and political bureaucracy, while hypothesizing what might happen to the nation's social institutions

THE SOUTH AFRICAN DELIMA

HIV/AIDS refers to the Human Immunodeficiency Virus and Acquired Immune Deficiency Syndrome respectively. *HIV* destroys the normal functioning of the immune system, which leads to the development of AIDS. This makes a person susceptible to infection and contraction of a myriad of other diseases. *HIV,* has been scientifically established as acquired through the transmission of "infected blood, semen, or vaginal secretions [that] come in contact with an uninfected person's broken skin or mucous membranes" (CDC 2003).

Currently Africa has the largest infection rate of *HIV/*AIDS of any continent in the world. Over 70 percent of world AIDS cases are from Africa, and 8,700 Africans are infected with HIV every minute- 3.2 million a year. The disease has greatly reduced the average life expectancy to around 40 years of age, and of the 25 million Africans infected, only an estimated 100,000 have access to antiretroviral drugs (World Bank 2002).

It has been argued that the affect that HIV/AIDS is having on Africa has little impact on the rest of the world. In North America, there are only an estimated 1.2 million cases, and in Western Europe, the numbers drop to less than 700,000. While much of the world may view HIV/AIDS as a tragedy little, besides monetary aid relief, is being accomplished to help African nations deal with the epidemic (World Bank 2002). However, it has also been opined that this epidemic obviously affects unemployment, economic policy and ultimately civil unrest.

This leaves few positive outcomes for sovereign states where unstable and corrupt regimes are normal; and while the rest of the continent faces an uncertain future, there is hope in the nation of South Africa. The rather peaceful end of segregation in 1994, and the limited corruption within the government, make it the best candidate for dealing with the epidemic, and gives it a greater chance for a positive outcome, though it will still be a significant challenge. South Africa has seen the number of infected double from 2.4 million in 1997 to over 5 million in 2004 (Hoyle 2004). As stated earlier, both men and women are equally infected, and it is expected that AIDS orphans will reach 2 million, with an expected 7 million AIDS deaths by the end of the decade (Butler 2004).

The nation also faces many of the same problems that the rest of southern Africa faces that contribute to the spread of the virus, such as the influx of migrant labor and prostitution. This produces large concentrations of young men in cities who later return to their families during holidays, or at the end of their contract. While in the cities they take part in the rampant prostitution and contract HIV, spreading it to their wives when they return home (Phillips 2004). In most African cities, the chance of contracting AIDS from a prostitute is 50 percent (Hoyle 2004). The success of prostitution and the spread of infection can be attributed to social norms within the different racial groups of South Africa.

All racial groups within the nation are being impacted by HIV/AIDS: the Blacks, Whites, Coloured, and Indians. Each racial group has dealt with the epidemic within their respective societies; however, the data shows that the Blacks have the highest percentage of prevalence within the nation (Avert.org 2005). This is due to their social practices regarding sex.

The Black population is the majority in South Africa. The term "Black" describes natives of African descent who are further broken up into tribes such as: Zulu, Xhosa, and Khoikhoi. As a whole, however, they share similar customs and ideals, and so will be grouped under one heading (Thompson 2000).

Blacks are the oldest inhabitants of South Africa, and only came into contact with White settlers in the sixteenth century. While each tribe has a diversified history with White settlers, they have all been used as slaves, uprooted from their homelands, and killed off. After the end of Apartheid segregation in 1994, the Blacks – through the ANC- reformed the government and became the political majority for the first time in over 300 years. Today the ANC is still the lead political party in South Africa (Thompson 2000).

Blacks currently have the highest HIV/AIDS infection rates in the nation. They account for over 76 percent of the population, have some of the highest birth rates, and an infection rate of 12.9 percent (Avert 2005). With a nation of over 42 million inhabitants, this means that the Black community makes up 4 million of the 5 million HIV/AIDS cases in South Africa (Butler 2004).

One main reason for the high infection rate is social behavior. AIDS awareness campaigns do not appeal to the Black community, especially because of the cultural acceptance of sexual relations. These campaigns have posted highway signs that read 'Choose life: Practice abstinence.' They try to promote 'behavior change' towards sex, yet have thus far only antagonized the situation. Some women enter into numerous sexual relationships to expel expectations of chastity, or for the gain of consumer items, despite the known risks. Social historians have also noticed that there is a "failure of communication between parents and children on sexual issues" (Carton 2003: 199).

There is also the cultural norm of "wife inheritance." When a woman is widowed, she is taken in by her husband's family for the care of herself, and her children. It is common that inheritors will then enter into sexual relations with this woman. If her husband died of AIDS, then the infected widow will spread the disease to her inheritor, who would then transmit the disease to his wife, who in turn could pass it on to breastfeeding children (Hoyle 2004).

Ignorance of the disease is another contributing factor to the spread of HIV amongst Blacks. One province known as Kwazulu-Natal, where the highest prevalence of the disease is found in South Africa amongst the Zulus, the term AIDS is referred to as the "woman's disease" since women are seen as sexually as promiscuous. A woman who discloses that she is infected faces the threat of being abandoned or killed (Albertyn 2003). This misguided social behavior only fuels the spread of HIV/AIDS amongst the Black community. Whites are the second largest racial group in South Africa. The term "Whites" incorporates the Afrikaners and English. While the two groups differ slightly in their religious and political beliefs, they are still very similar in their social attitude.

In yet another study published by Campbell, (Campbell 1999) Dr. Campbell along with her colleagues, determined the effects of relationships with the legal, medical, and mental health systems and how they affected a victim's psychological and mental health. Their conclusion from this study was also revealing because the results of that study indicated that "…although community services may be beneficial for some victims, there is increasing evidence that they can add trauma, rather than alleviate distress (termed secondary victimization)." (Campbell 1999). The author illustrated the effects of secondary victimization on survivors' posttraumatic stress (PTS) symptoms.

In Campbell's study, samples were used to recruit over one hundred survivors. According to Campbell, et. al, "...victims of non-stranger rape who received minimal assistance from either the legal or medical system, and encountered victim-blaming behaviors from system personnel, had significantly elevated levels of PTS." (Campbell 1999) Such re-victimization is counterproductive because if the mission of specific agencies is to de traumatize and assist victims with rehabilitative therapy, post-traumatic stress levels should not be much greater than other victims in their study, particularly victims who did not seek help from a variety of agencies.

Apparently, the authors' infer that high-risk survivors who receive sustained services had a decrease over time in post-traumatic symptoms. Thus, the question raised is not only what type of services is being offered, but also the length of time the assistance is proffered along with the nature and quality of service. Furthermore, "...although community services may be beneficial for some victims, there is increasing evidence that they can add trauma, rather than alleviate distress (termed secondary victimization)." (Id.) This article illustrated the effects of secondary victimization on survivors' posttraumatic stress (PTS) symptoms. A sample of over one hundred rape victims were engaged in this study. According to Campbell, et. al, "...victims ...who received minimal assistance from either the legal or medical system, and encountered victim-blaming behaviors from system personnel, had significantly elevated levels of PTS." (Id.)

In conclusion, research revealed that if the goal was to assist victims with rehabilitative services, then it would follow that subsequent PST levels would not be greater than other victims in their analysis, particularly victims who did not ask for aid from a variety of social service agencies. Apparently, the authors' infer that high-risk survivors who receive sustained services had a decrease over time in post-traumatic symptoms. Thus, the question raised is not only what type of service is being offered, but also the length of time the assistance is proffered along with the nature and quality of service. PST is still commonplace among citizens of South Africa who experienced apartheid and its repercussions.

The history of the White population begins with the arrival of the Dutch East- Indian Company. South Africa became a colony of the Company in 1652 and acted as a supplying post for ships passing through to Asia. In 1795, the British assumed power and Whites were able to expand further into the region through superior technology, economics, and pitting tribes against each other (Butler 2004). In 1910, South Africa became its own country, and in 1948, the Afrikaners gained control of the government with their Nationalist Party (NP). They were then able to slowly eliminate all Black and colored people's participation in the political system through the policy of Apartheid, or separation of the races (Thompson 2000).

Whites currently have an infection rate far below that of Blacks. They account for about 11 percent of the population, and have a group infection rate of just over 6 percent. This means the White population has 280,000 HIV/AIDS cases. Their lower infection rate can be attributed to their social behavior and attitudes towards sex (Avert 2005).

White social norms prevent them from being sexually promiscuous due to European based religious beliefs that promote abstinence. They have always held the positions of economic and political power in South Africa, which has allowed them to finance proper educations for their children, which have aided them in the teaching of proper moral behavior. They are overwhelmingly Christian with strong Calvinist beliefs within the Dutch Reformed Church.

If the current rate of infection continues amongst Whites, their society will see little change. Even after their change in economic and social standing, Whites have continued to be a powerful force in South Africa. Their infection rates are low, and their religious beliefs do not allow for promiscuity.

The term "Coloured" is used to describe the section of the population that is a mixture of different races. They are mostly found in the Cape area, and after emancipation from slavery in 1834, they began to refer to themselves as the Cape Coloured People. Up until 1857, the Coloured were incorporated into Afrikaner society and suffered minimal discrimination. However, pressure from the Dutch Reformed Church forced the beginnings of segregation and a split of the congregation, leading to the establishment of the Uniting Reformed Church for Coloured participation. Coloureds are a very diverse group, both culturally and economically. The formation of the Union of South Africa in 1910 legalized discrimination against Coloureds, which made it difficult for them to compete with Whites for positions (Thompson 2000).

The infection rates amongst the Coloured population are similar to those of the Whites. They constitute 9 percent of the population, and have an infection rate similar to Whites at just over 6 percent. This puts their total population infected at 225,000 (Avert 2005).

The lower rates amongst Coloured compared to Blacks could be associated with their social/cultural similarities to the White population. Despite the prejudice and discrimination they faced after 1910, the long history of being economically and socially similar to Whites became imbedded in their culture. The similarity in culture was also reflected in their similar White sexual attitudes. If the current rate of infection amongst Coloureds continues, their society will see little change (Thompson 2000).

The Indian population is the smallest group in South Africa, and also the newest migrant group. Their population began to flourish in South Africa in the 1860s when the British government began to import them from India to resolve a skilled labor shortage. They are mostly found in on the east coast, especially within the city of Durban where there is a large Indian-based community (Thompson 2000).

The Indian population currently has the lowest infection rates of any group in South Africa. They compose only 3 percent of the population, and have an infection rate of less than 2 percent. This means their infected population stands at only 16,000 people (Avert 2005).

Their low infection rates may be a result of their social behavior with regards to sex. Traditional Hindu beliefs discourage sex before marriage, and it is estimated that 60 percent of men are virgins on their wedding nights. Sex and children are viewed as a stage in life, and the act of adultery can reflect on a person's karma. Although some Indians have changed their religious beliefs (40 percent follow other faiths), imbedded cultural norms are more difficult to alter (Richards 2004). If the Indian infection rate continues to remain below 2 percent, their group will see little impact of the AIDS epidemic.

If South Africa does not deal with the problem of HIV/AIDS, there is the possibility of economic and political instability within the next few decades. A generation gap in the population due to the HIV/AIDS epidemic could result in the prior of these two. Currently the population is undergoing negative population growth due to AIDS. The majority of HIV cases are amongst the reproductive population from the ages of 20-34; which may lead to a generation gap. This generation gap could have a dramatic impact on South Africa within the next few decades, which could lead to lack of skilled employees in the nation, leading to a damaged economy. "As a quarter of skilled workers and perhaps one in seven highly skilled workers become infected by 2005, AIDS will also severely undermine the human capital in the public service, business, and the professions that will be required to address the pandemic's consequences" (Butler 2004: 144). With a lack of opportunities in the job market, a large portion of the professional community has left in search for opportunities in other nations such as Australia, the UK, Canada, and the US. More than 200,000 emigrated in the 1990s, and it is estimated that this number will double by 2010 (Butler 2004). Should this trend continue, the combination of emigrated and dead skilled workers could bring about an economic crisis.

A second generation gap could appear through the loss of children. Those who are breast fed from their infected mothers have a one in third chance of contracting the virus if the mother is not taking azidothymidine (AZT) retroviral drugs (Hoyle 2004). Current access to AZT drugs is limited in South Africa with only 1.4 million people currently receiving treatment. Often, it is unknown whether or not a child has been infected by his dead mother, and the child is abandoned (Sidley 2003).

Economic instability within African nations tends to lead to corruption, as can be seen in neighboring Zimbabwe. Its drastic economic decline over the last two decades has turned the nation into an autocratic regime. Though this is a faint possibility for South Africa, there will undoubtedly be a change within its society due to the AIDS epidemic.

The religious community has tried to help bring about AIDS awareness through reaching out to the community. They have a history of community service, and has served in South Africa as a mediator between colonizers and Blacks. When Coloured children were banned from public school is 1857, mission institutions opened their doors to educating them (Thompson 2000).

The two largest religious organizations are the Zion Christian Church, with over 4 million members, and the Dutch Reformed Churches, with a combined membership of almost 4 million. The latter was considered to be the national religion during apartheid and followed the NP political agenda. Many religious organizations, such as the

Methodist Church, Catholic Church, and Anglican Church aided in the end of apartheid, although many members left the Catholic and Anglican Churches in support of apartheid policies (Butler 2004).

Today these religious organizations try to educate the population on the hazards of HIV/AIDS. This can be seen through the growing Zion Christian Church that accepts the traditional beliefs of the Africans, and as a result has built a large following since 1990. They condemn the consumption of alcoholic beverages, smoking, sexual promiscuity, and violence (Butler 2004). The Catholic Church also condemns sexual promiscuity, and is against the government handing out condoms. The Anglican Church has taken this stance on condoms as well, and in January 2005, they announced the beginning of "Teaching Our Children" program which is aimed at teaching abstinence amongst the younger generations (iafrica 2005b)

No matter what the current program against AIDS in South Africa is, the current rate of infection will lead to a shift in the nation's society. This could lead to a shift in the nation's political structure since history shows-through the example of apartheid- that social turmoil leads to political change.

Apartheid began in 1948 when Afrikaner nationalists came to power. The program encouraged "separate development of the races" which lead to the placement of Blacks into homelands (Tordoff 2002, 65).

In places where the African nationalist movement was able to flourish, the African social upheaval against townships and segregation policies led to the eventual fall of apartheid and a change in the government's structure (Tordoff 2002). The government today is still headed by the ANC; however, their attempts to control the epidemic have not been successful. They are viewed both domestically and internationally as being inept. The following will examine the government's successes and failures.

The transition of power in 1994 delayed the response time to the outbreak of the virus, and has resulted in some questionable policymaking with regards to HIV/AIDS. During the first few years of the new government, President Mandela desegregated the prisons' infected from uninfected, and began the distribution of condoms to all prisoners. The policy of prison segregation, under the apartheid regime, controlled the outbreak of AIDS within the prisons; however, since the ANC was desegregating the rest of society, it only goes to follow that this course of action would extend to all aspects of government services. The ANC had a different stance on AIDS compared to the Afrikaners, and even "overturned the policy of the police, correctional services and defense force to carry out HIV testing on all new applicants for jobs" (Phillips 2004: 42). Whites were concerned about the disease, and even went so far as to test their Black workers for fear they might infect family members. Meanwhile, young Black activists considered the virus another propaganda ploy by the government in the last days of apartheid to stop the African nationalist movement. Some even called AIDS the acronym for "Afrikaner Invention to Deprive us of Sex," and Blacks paid little heed to the disease (Phillips 2004: 34).

Since the end of capital punishment, the integration of infected prisoners is a dangerous choice. Many incarcerated individuals have not even gone to trial yet to decide their fate. Approximately 23 percent of those being held are still in the pre-trial phase. If set free, these innocent people have possibly contracted the AIDS virus, and could reenter society and infect more of the population (Human 2004). Crime in general has risen since the transition of power, and South Africa is one of the largest rape capitals of the world. From September 2002 to August 2003, almost 23 percent of South Africans reported being a victim of crime.

Secondary victimization has been defined by one criminologist, R. Campbell, in her article entitled, "Secondary victimization of rape victims: insights from mental health professionals who treat survivors of violence." Secondary victimization has been determined to be a repercussion of repeated instances of is frequently the result of the shock of sexual incursions of abuse or rape victims. The article illustrates that such repeated disturbances is a secondary repercussion of several types of assaults which happens through the responses of individuals and institutions to the victim. There are many types of secondary victimization. These include but are not limited to victim blaming, inappropriate behavior or language by medical personnel and by other organizations with access to the victim post assault. (See, Campbell 1989) Several studies have indicated that many survivors may be receiving benign forms of assistance from the criminal justice system but these same survivors become ill-treated by the same agencies whose mission is to help victims. In one particular study conducted by Dr. Campbell, a probability sampling was used to survey a representative sample of licensed mental health professionals about the extent to which they believe rape victims are subjected to destructive and/or violent and abusive behavior in their interactions with social system personnel. Campbell's findings are startling. Research revealed that many health care professionals actually engage in harmful behavior detrimental to the "victim." (Campbell, 1999)

It is estimated that more than half of the crime that takes place is actually reported (Burton 2004). In 2000, there were over 50,000 rape cases reported, and if this accounts for only half, then it can be assumed that over 100,000 cases of rape actually took place (Amnesty 2003). This would also put South Africa's crime rate from September 2002 to August 2003 at over 46 percent (Burton 2004).

While these changes to policy and society may be seen as destructive to South Africa, the ANC has tried multiple tactics to educate the people of South Africa to prevent such damage. Upon entering the office of Presidency, Mandela doubled the government budget for AIDS Awareness programs, extended them to public schools, began condom distribution, and increased media attention. The ANC also stopped the testing of HIV/AIDS amongst incoming hospital patients, since it was seen as an infringement to human rights which could prevent someone from obtaining proper medical care (Phillips 2004: 42).

However, the cycle has begun again, and President Mbeki is now facing the same criticisms Mandela did. Mbeki is seen as not supporting intellectual property rights in his attempt to bring in AZT drugs to South Africa. In 2001, 39 pharmaceutical companies took the government to court over legislation that would give the government the power to manufacture generics of brand-name drugs. The cost in 2001 for the combination of drugs needed to treat the disease was over $1,000 a month per patient (BBC 2001). Other options are available to the government besides the procurement of expensive AZT drugs, such as basic vitamin supplements, which some studies have shown can also reduce the chance of transmission, although even these have become hard to come by (Bering 2000). The drug companies eventually dropped their case, and under the Trade Related Aspects of Intellectual Property Rights, the government can produce and sell products with patents without the compliance of the patent holder (Barrow 2001). While this allows cheap drugs to be distributed and possibly curtail the spread of infection, it also prevents companies from investing in South Africa-especially those with patents they would like to protect.

In 2000, President Thabo Mbeki stated to the world that he did not consider AIDS to be the largest health threat facing South Africa, and doubted HIV even caused AIDS. He cited poorer socio-economic classes as being the contributing factor since they have higher infection rate. This statement lead to African AIDS activists and the Congress of South African Trade Unions to threaten a civil disobedience campaign should the government not discuss the provision of AZT drugs (Hunter 2003). It is true that those from lower incomes tend to have more risky sexual experiences, diminished access to health information which can lead to a delayed diagnosis and treatment, and lowered concern about one's future health; however, it is more likely Mbeki was playing a political game (Fassin 2003). The government views AIDS differently than it views other diseases, such as malaria. The South African government sees malaria as curable, and therefore worth the cost of prevention, generally through the use of DDT sprays. In contrast, HIV/AIDS is a disease that can be hidden from the infected individual, and most importantly, is not curable (Bering 2000).

Even if the government did show full support towards aiding HIV/AIDS patients, it could never afford to provide its entire infected population with AZT drugs. If South Africa were to purchase AZT retroviral drugs, it would use up the entire public health budget of the nation – and that only accounts for those patients that have admitted to being infected with HIV/AIDS. While the number stands at 5 million, in reality, the numbers could be much higher (Bering 2000).

Current supplies of antiviral drugs are being poorly distributed in South Africa. There have even been cases of child rape victims not having access to AZT drugs because they are not available. It is especially difficult for children (who account for 40 percent of rape victims) to obtain the drugs since parental permission is needed (BBC 2004). However, distribution today is far better than in the 1990s when the ANC government blocked the use of antiretroviral drugs due to their concern for possible side- effects, and refused to give pregnant women drugs even though AZT was proven "to be effective at staving off the fatal complications of the virus" (Moeller 2000: 89). More than half of HIV positive women choose to carry their pregnancy to term (Plessis 2003). This treatment has been proven to greatly reduce the transmission of HIV from mother to child through pregnancy and breastfeeding, which accounts for 10% of the annual infection rates (Makgoba 2000).

Children that do not acquire the virus from their mothers, whom die, end up becoming orphans. The government has acknowledged the need to care and provide for AIDS orphans, but currently the programs in place are limited, and are only a temporary solution with no long-term goals.

This continued growth of orphans is a dangerous situation. The current social response to this is family adoption. Blacks have a tradition known as Ubuntu where the relatives or even neighbors will see to the child's basic needs. However, there is a stigma attached to children orphaned by AIDS, and they are often times ostracized by society, even if they are not infected. Those who are not taken in by family are often forced to fend for themselves. Young girls begin prostituting, and boys join gangs and add to South Africa's colossal crime rates. The government currently has a Foster Care Grant in place which distributes R410 ($66 USD) monthly to foster parents willing to take in orphans to AIDS parents. Unfortunately, the system can take up to two years to distribute money to families in need (Landman 2002).

The most difficult issue the government faces in order to control the spread of AIDS is the changing of social norms regarding sex. Perhaps, the Black's view on sex which has lead to their highest infection rate compared to other groups. Indians, who have a very strict cultural view on sex, have the least amount of infection. A solution is needed that will set up domestic programs which will focus on behavior modification towards sexual attitudes.

The solution to the AIDS epidemic in South Africa currently being implemented by the government is one of plausible denial. Thabo Mbeki's 2000 speech, addressed to the world, stated that he did not believe that HIV caused AIDS. In 1998, the ANC government blocked the use of antiretroviral drugs, due to their concern for possible side- effects. If the government argues the facts behind AIDS and its treatments, then it has no need support possible treatments; for example, they would not have to provide AZT drugs if they deny that HIV causes AIDS.

Their current solution allows the government to put off its responsibility to the people, has damaged its image abroad, and has prevented outside donors who are reluctant to back HIVIAIDS programs when the leadership of South Africa is seen as questioning known treatments. Recently, the government changed its tune and began the distribution of AZT drugs to 1.4 million of the 5 million infected. However, this does little to stop the growth of the epidemic, and it is estimated that another 400,000 people will become infected before the program finishes its first year (Sidley 2003).

This solution will not solve the HIV/AIDS crisis in South Africa, and has the nation heading towards disaster. With the expectation that AIDS orphans will reach 2 million, and the AIDS death toll will reach 7 million by 2010, there will be considerable social and economic turmoil (Butler 2004).

The best solution for South Africa's future is to come to an understanding that nothing can be done to help those infected, but the future can still be stabilized through tough government action that calls for a change to current AIDS awareness programs and an attempt to teach behavior modification rather than simply passing out condoms and condoning promiscuous sexual relationships. The promotion of abstinence should be the government's key campaign against HIVIAIDS. This solution will affect the nations: economics, crime, drug provisions, social behavior and sexual attitudes, and provide an answer for dealing with the inevitable 2 million orphans. This solution will also focus the government on long-term containment of HIV/AIDS, while trying to prevent the nation from going bankrupt.

The problem with this solution is that it is not the most humanitarian method. Since the government will fundamentally be ignoring the impending deaths of 5 million of its citizens it is likely the international community - mostly the western world - will see this solution as barbaric. At the same time though, perhaps the South African government will finally gain some respect for being rational about the disease.

There is also the chance that this solution will fail, in which case the nation will be left with millions of orphans without social guidance and further add to domestic problems. The economy could never recover from the deaths of skilled labor, and could fall into further disarray. Crime, which has become a normal occurrence within the nation, could continue to run rampant, even after the changes have been implemented. Lastly, there is the chance that sexual behavior changes could fail and the Black community could continue with lax sexual attitudes, thus continuing the transmission cycle.

However, with this solution, once the government realizes it cannot save the 5 million infected, they will be able to focus their resources on providing for the future stability of South Africa. The first step is to begin improvements to the nation's economic structure. "While citizens have remained sympathetic towards the government's difficulties in extending public services, the lack of employment opportunities has been a matter of profound and growing dissatisfaction for South Africans of all classes" (Butler 2004: 62). After the change in government in 1994, the nation has seen slow economic growth accompanied by steady population growth (Butler 2004). Incentives to new industry and foreign investors could bring the much-needed business into South Africa.

The government should rethink its stance on its intellectual property rights laws in order to bring in foreign investors. Unfortunately, the current crime rate is keeping many skilled laborers out of South Africa, and until something is done about this, it is unlikely the emigrated and skilled South Africans will return. Crime and economics are mixed and, theoretically, once job opportunities become available to the masses, crime will begin to fall.

Next, the solution would call for a re-education of the population on sexual attitudes and behaviors, and how AIDS awareness is taught. The current sexual norms within the Black community will only further impede the challenge against HN/AIDS. However, as seen in Uganda, these norms can be changed. The country was able to reduce its infection rate from 29 percent to fewer than 5 percent within a decade. Their government did not distribute condoms, as South Africa does; instead, they focused on campaigning abstinence (iafrica 2005a). The distribution of condoms only negates any attempt at promoting abstinence, and gives the appearance that condoms are the foolproof method of preventing transmission, when in fact it is still under debate at just how effective they are. By changing the populations attitude through new awareness campaigns there would be a lower infection rate, which would help curtail the cycle of transmission.

Stopping transmission would be further aided by the government giving AZT drug priority to breastfeeding mothers. They should be given priority access to drugs, in order to prevent the spread of disease to their children. These orphaned children should be given the attention they need to prevent them from enter into lives of crime and prostitution. Current programs for foster children in place are limited, funding of only $66 a month, and delay in money distribution needs to be expanded upon to deal with the coming 2 million orphans. The program should provide more money and resources, in a timely manner, to those providing foster care. More orphanages should be established, both private and state-run, to raise and educate AIDS orphans. Establishing these organizations would allow the government or community organizations to give each child a chance at an education and modify cultural behavior.

Sexual behavior modification could be further aided by setting up programs to rid stigmas attached to HIVIAIDS victims and their children. Mandela has taken a lead role in the awareness of AIDS in South Africa. The recent death of his son due to AIDS, and his outreach into the AIDS community, has been instrumental in awareness. Slowly he and others are changing the stigmas associated with AIDS.

This solution, should it succeed, will provide the government with a stable future consisting of changed social norms regarding sex, and a generation of children raised by the state. It will allow the government to accept that those infected cannot be cured, but future generations can benefit from proper HIV/AIDS awareness.

The HIV/AIDS epidemic is slowly destroying the nation of South Africa. With over 5 million currently infected, and the numbers rising each year, the government has made little attempt to curb the outbreak, and at times has been seen as an inhibitor. With the lack of resources to deal with the disease and its consequences, and the high infection rates amongst the Black community, there will be a major upheaval in the structure of South African society as an entire generation is allowed to die, and millions more are allowed to become infected.

South Africa currently has over 5 million people infected with HIV/AIDS and over 4 million of those are from the sizable Black community. Other racial groups within the society, such as the Whites, Coloureds, and Indians, have a much lower percentage of infected within their communities. This is due to social attitudes regarding sexuality. Blacks are more sexually open and promiscuous, and therefore have higher rates. The other groups have imbedded attitudes that support abstinence.

The South African government has tried futilely to contain the epidemic through sexual programs that are aimed at teaching "safe sex" through condom use. They have also implemented policies that seem to only aid the virus in spreading, such as integration of HIV positive prisoners with non-infected prisoners. The new policy that gives the government access to product patents, for the production of cheap AZT drugs, has kept international investment into South Africa low, as has the high national crime rates. Current production of AZT drugs is very low, and does not give priority to breastfeeding mothers. They have a one-in-three chance of infecting their breastfeeding children.

The most feasible solution for the government of South Africa is to understand that nothing can be done to help those currently infected, and switch awareness programs to promote behavioral changes in sexual attitudes, rather than condoning promiscuity. The government should also focus its attention to the 2 million AIDS orphans that are expected before 2010. These children could easily turn to lives of crime or prostitution, but with the correct foster care in place, they could have productive futures within South African society. The ability for the government to access national patents should be revoked to allow for further international investment and, hopefully, an increase in the economy. With this increase in economy, crime rates should theoretically fall.

This solution, however, could fail. It could give the government a negative image internationally since it will fundamentally be ignoring the impending deaths of 5 million of its citizens. There is also the chance that the orphan programs will fail, in which case the nation will be left with millions of children without social guidance and further add to domestic problems. There is the possibility that the economy would not turn for the better, and crime rates could continue to grow. Finally, there is the chance that behavior modification will not take hold within the Black community, and the epidemic will continue to grow.

Even with this said, this last solution is the nation's best hope. It has been tested and proven in Uganda were the country was able to reduce its infection rate from 29 percent to fewer than 5 percent within a decade. Their government did not distribute condoms, as South Africa does; instead, they focused on campaigning abstinence. They faced all the same troubles South Africa currently does, and were able to overcome the epidemic.

This paper was not intended to fully penetrate the sexual and social attitudes of each group. Other explanations could be given for lower infection rates within some groups, especially that of the Coloureds who are in limbo between White and Blacks. An extensive study could be performed on each of these groups further. However, this Thesis does explain, in detail, Black social norms and gives good examples of traditions that have facilitated the infection rate amongst the group.

The following are problematic issues that have been marshaled during the process of this paper:

- What does recent research say about Blacks being more easily infected with HIV/AIDS than Whites?
- What would be the estimated population of each racial group with current growing infection rates and infant mortality for 2025?
- How is White emigration affecting future prospects of the nation?
- What types of companies have expressed their concern over South Africa's patent laws, and have they declined entering into business in the nation due to them?

WORKS CITED

Albertyn, C. (2003). Contesting democracy: *HNI*AIDS and the achievement of gender equality in South Africa. [electronic version] *Feminist Studies, 29(3),* 595-616

Amnesty. (2003). Amnesty International. Amnesty International Report: South Africa. [electronic version] Retrieved on April17, 2005 from http://web.amnesty.org/web/web.nsf/report2003/zaf-summary- eng/$FILE/south%20africa.pdf

ANC. (2004, 24 March). African National Congress. Maps Index. Retrieved on April18, 2005 from http://www.anc.org.zallists/maplist.html

Avert. (2005, 21 March). South Africa HIVIAIDS statistics. Retrieved on March 26, 2005 from http://www.avert.org/safricastats.htm

Barrow, G. (2001, 19 April). BBC News. *Cheaper drugs a long way off.* Retrieved on March 28, 2005 from http://news.bbc.co.uk/1/hi/world/africa/1285616.stm

BBC. (2001, 19 April). BBC News. *SA victory in AIDS drugs case.* Retrieved on March 28, 2005 from http://news.bbc.co.uk/1/hilworld/africa/1285097.stm

BBC. (2004, 4 March). BBC News. *SA 'failing rape victims on AIDS.* Retrieved on March 28, 2005 from http://news.bbc.co.uk/1/hi/world/africa/3532071.stm

Bering, H. (2000, May). *AIDS in South Africa.* The Washington Times, pp. 15

Burton, P.; duPlessis, A.; Leggettt,T.; Louw,A.; Mistry,D.; and van Vuuren, H. (2004, July). Institute for Security Studies. Crime levels in South Africa. [electronic version] Retrieved on March 28, 2005 from http://www.iss.co.zalpubs/Monographs/No101/Chap6.htm

Butler, A. (2004). Contemporary South Africa. New York: Palgrave Macmillian. Carton, B. (2003). The forgotten compass of death: Apocalypse then and now in the social history of South Africa. The Journal of Social History, 37 (1), 1999

Campbell R, Raja S. (1999) Secondary victimization of rape victims: insights from mental health professionals who treat survivors of violence. Violence Vict. 14(3):261-75.

CDC. (2005, 17 February). Center for Disease Control. Frequently asked questions on HIVIAIDS.

Retrieved on March 28, 2005 from http://www.cdc.gov/hiv/pubs/faqs.htm#definition

Fassin, D. & Schneider, H. (2003, 1 March). The politics of AIDS in South Africa: Beyond the
     controversies. British Medical Journal (International edition), 326 (7387), 495-498.

Hattendorf, J., & Tollerud, T.R. (1997). Domestic Violence: Counseling Strategies That Minimize the
     Impact of Secondary Victimization. Journal Perspectives in Psychiatric Care, 33(1), 14-23

Hoyle, B. (2004). AIDSIHIV. Farmington Hills, MI: The Gale Group.

Human Rights Watch. (1994, 1 February). Prison Conditions in South Africa. [electronic version]
     Human Rights Watch.

Hunter, S. (2003). Black Death: AIDS in Africa. New York, NY: Palgrave Macmillian. iafrica. (2005,
     24 January). iafrica.com. Condom strategy 'clearly not working'. Retrieved on March 28, 2005.
     http://africa.iafrica.com/pls/procs/SEARCH.ARCHIVE?p_content_id=367495&p site id=2

iafrica. (2005b, 12 January). iafrica.com. Church to launch $10m HIV/Aids plan. Retrieved on March
     28, 2005 from
     http://africa.iafrica.com/pls/procs/SEARCH.ARCHIVE?p_content_id=159792&p site id=2

Landman, C. (2002, Nov). The AIDS Orphans of South Africa. Contemporary Review, 281 (1642),
     268.

Makogba, M. (2000, 19 May). HIV/AIDS: The peril of pseudoscience. Science, 288 (5469), 1171.

McCubbins, M. D. and Thies, M. F. (1996). Rationality and the Foundations of Positive Political
     Theory. [Online] Available: http://polisciexplab.ucsd.edu/mccubbin/current/ratcho.htm

Moeller, S. (Fall2000). Coverage of AIDS in Africa: The media are silent no longer. Nieman Reports,
     54 (3), 89.

Phillips, H. (2004). HIV/AIDS in the context of South Africa's epidemic history. In Kauffman, K. &
     Lindauer, D. (Ed.) (2004). AIDS and South Africa: The social expression of a pandemic.
     Wellesley, MA: Palgrave Macmillian.

Plessis, G. (2003). HIV and fertility in South Africa: Some theoretical and methodological considerations. Department of Social Development. (2003). Fertility: Current South African issues of poverty, HIV/AIDS & youth. Cape Town, South Africa: HSRC Publishers.

Richards, S. (2004). Faithnet. Hindu attitudes to sex. Retrieved on March 28, 2005 from http://www.faithnet.org.uk/KS4/Marriage%20and%20the%20Familylhindusex.ht m

Sidley, P. (2003). South Africa introduces the world's largest AIDS treatment plan. British Medical Journal, 327 (7426), 1246.

Thompson, L. (2000). A History of South Africa. (3rd ed.). USA: Yale University Press.

Tordoff, W. (2002). Government and politics in Africa. (4th ed.). Bloomington, IN: Indiana University Press.

TravelSource (n.d). Retrieved March 28, 2005 from http://www.travelsource.nl/story/africa/zawolt/zuidafrika.asp?travelreportid=46& destinationid=501

World Bank. (2002). World Bank Group. Intensifying action against HIVIAIDS in Africa. Retrieved on April 2, 2005 from http://www.worldbank.org/afr/aids/overview.htm

APPENDIX

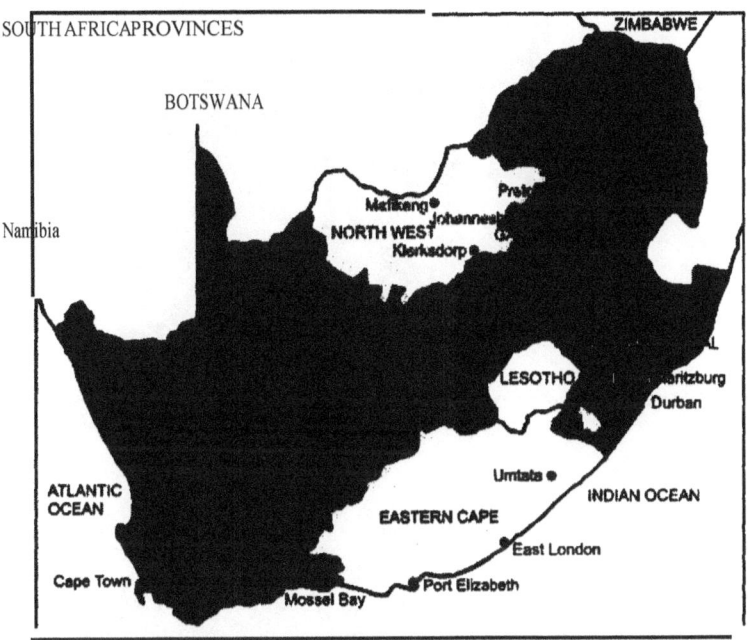

Figure 2: Provinces of South Africa. (Source: ANC, 2004)

Figure 3: Thabo Mbeki, Nelson Mandela, and F.W. de Klerk. (Source: South Africa Travel, 2005).

Figure 4: The South African Flag. (Travel Source, n.d.).